Pebble Plus

Weather Basics

Wind

by Erin Edison
Consulting Editor: Gail Saunders-Smith, PhD

CAPSTONE PRESS
a capstone imprint

Pebble Plus is published by Capstone Press,
1710 Roe Crest Drive, North Mankato, Minnesota 56003.
www.capstonepub.com

Copyright © 2012 by Capstone Press, a Capstone imprint. All rights reserved.
No part of this publication may be reproduced in whole or in part, or stored in a retrieval system, or transmitted in any form or by any means, electronic, mechanical, photocopying, recording, or otherwise, without written permission of the publisher. For information regarding permission, write to Capstone Press,
1710 Roe Crest Drive, North Mankato, Minnesota 56003.

Library of Congress Cataloging-in-Publication Data
Edison, Erin.
  Wind / by Erin Edison.
     p. cm.—(Pebble plus. Weather basics)
  Summary: "Simple text and full-color photographs describe wind and how it affects weather"—Provided by publisher.
  Includes bibliographical references and index.
  ISBN 978-1-4296-6054-9 (library binding)
  ISBN 978-1-4296-7082-1 (paperback)
  ISBN 978-1-4296-8756-0 (saddle-stitch)
  1. Winds—Juvenile literature. I. Title. II. Series.
  QC931.4.E35 2012
  551.51'8—dc22   2010053974

Editorial Credits
Erika L. Shores, editor; Kyle Grenz, designer; Laura Manthe, production specialist

Photo Credits
Image courtesy of Earth Sciences and Image Analysis Laboratory, NASA Johnson Space Center, 13
Shutterstock: Darren Baker, 5, David Steele, 21, George Bailey, 15, Gregory Johnston, back cover, JOANCHANG, cover, Marty Ellis, 19, Peter Wey, 9, Petronilo G. Dangoy Jr., 7, Poznyakov, 1, Ramon Berk, 17, Zastol`skiy Victor Leonidovich, 11

Artistic Effects
Shutterstock: marcus55

Capstone Press thanks Mike Shores, earth science teacher at RBA Public Charter School in Mankato, Minnesota, for his assistance on this book.

Note to Parents and Teachers

The Weather Basics series supports national science standards related to earth science. This book describes and illustrates wind. The images support early readers in understanding the text. The repetition of words and phrases helps early readers learn new words. This book also introduces early readers to subject-specific vocabulary words, which are defined in the Glossary section. Early readers may need assistance to read some words and to use the Table of Contents, Glossary, Read More, Internet Sites, and Index sections of the book.

Table of Contents

What Is Wind?......... 4
Wind and Weather.... 8
Kinds of Wind....... 12
We Need the Wind .. 18

Glossary............... 22
Read More 23
Internet Sites......... 23
Index 24

What Is Wind?

What pushes sailboats

across the water?

What rustles tree leaves?

It's moving air, called wind.

Sunlight warms air unevenly. Cool air sinks. Warm air rises. These air movements are wind.

Wind and Weather

Wind affects the weather.

It moves rain clouds.

Rain falls on the land

and water below.

Tornadoes and hurricanes are storms with extreme winds. These storms cause major damage.

Kinds of Wind

Global winds blow air over large parts of Earth. Jet streams are long ribbons of powerful global winds. Storms follow paths made by jet streams.

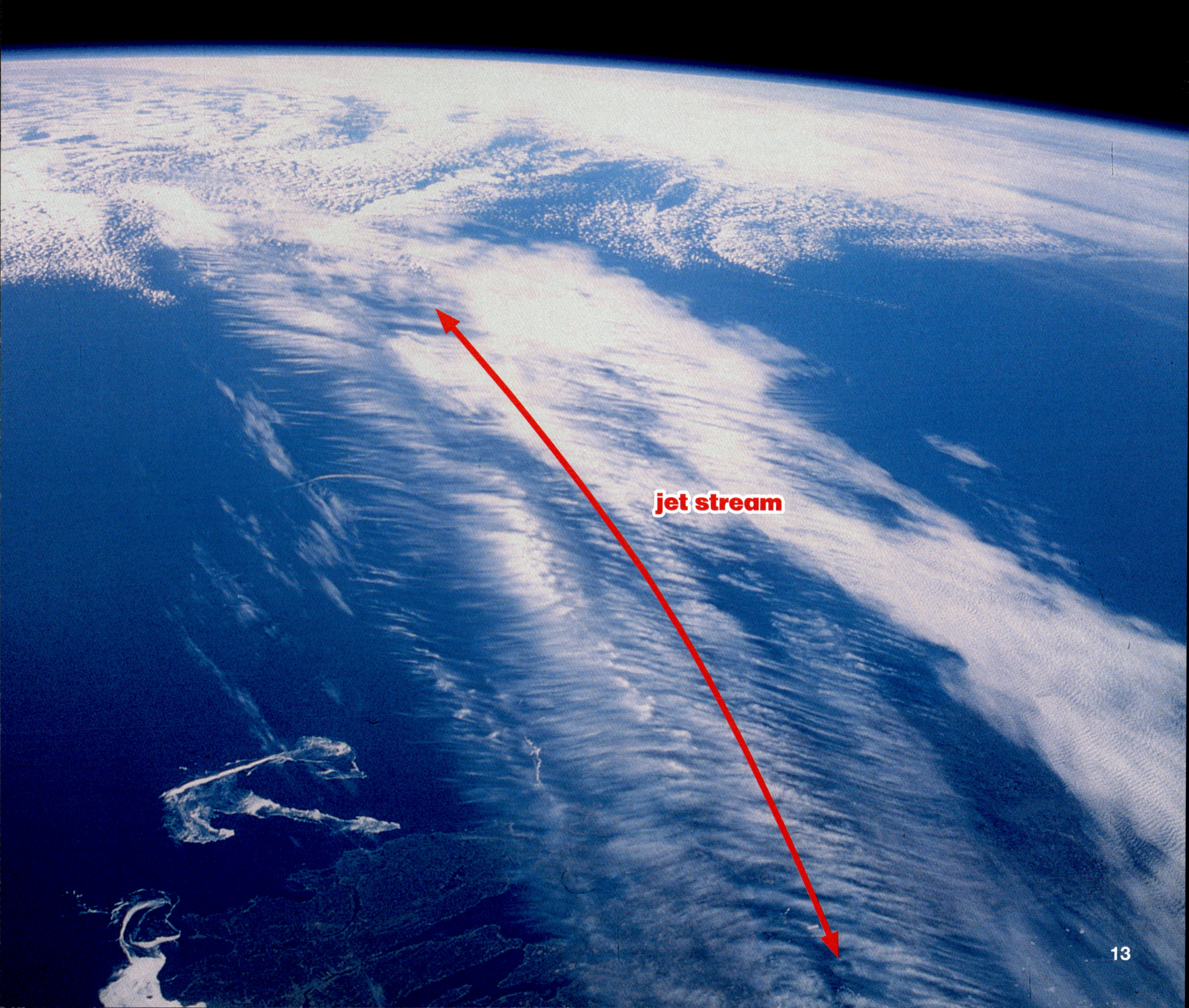

Local winds blow only short distances.

Winds that move kites and toss leaves are local winds.

A light local wind is a breeze.
It moves grass. A very strong
local wind is a gale.
Gales bend trees
and break branches.

We Need the Wind

Wind helps plants and animals. Birds fly faster and farther because of wind. Wind carries seeds and pollen.

People use wind turbines to catch wind. The wind turns blades to make electricity. Wind turbines help people use the power of wind.

Glossary

breeze—a gentle wind

gale—a very strong wind

global—something that happens throughout the world

jet stream—a fast-moving current of wind that blows from west to east around Earth

local—having to do with a small area

pollen—tiny grains that flowers produce

rustle—to move together and make a soft, crackling sound

wind turbine—an engine that is driven by propellers and uses energy from the wind to make electricity

Read More

Greene, Carol. *Please, Wind?* Rookie Ready to Learn. New York: Children's Press, 2011.

Sterling, Kristin. *It's Windy Today.* What's the Weather Like? Minneapolis: Lerner Publications Co., 2010.

Internet Sites

FactHound offers a safe, fun way to find Internet sites related to this book. All of the sites on FactHound have been researched by our staff.

Here's all you do:

Visit *www.facthound.com*

Type in this code: 9781429660549

Index

animals, 18
breezes, 16
clouds, 8
electricity, 20
gales, 16
global winds, 12
hurricanes, 10
jet streams, 12
kites, 14

leaves, 4, 14
local winds, 14, 16
plants, 16, 18
rain, 8
sailboats, 4
storms, 10, 12
sunlight, 6
tornadoes, 10
wind turbines, 20

Word Count: 165
Grade: 1
Early-Intervention Level: 17